BENJAMIN ZEPHANIAH

A Biography - The Untold Truth of His Life, TV Roles, Writings, Family Background, Awards, and Death

Linda Harrell

All rights reserved. No part of this publication may be reproduced, distributed,or transmitted in any form or by any means, including photocopying, recording, or other electronic or mechanical methods, without the prior written permission of the publisher, except in the case of brief quotations embodied in critical reviews and certain other noncommercial uses permitted by copyright law.

Copyright © Linda Harrell, 2023.

Table of Content

Introduction

Chapter 1

   Early Life and Background
- Childhood and Family
- Influences and Inspirations

Chapter 2

   Journey into Poetry
- Discovery of Poetry
- Development of Dub Poetry

Chapter 3

   Literary Contributions
- Notable Works:
- Style and Themes:

Chapter 4

   Musical Pursuits
- Integration of Poetry with Reggae
- Impact on the Music Scene

Chapter 5

   Personal Life
- Relationships and Family
- Personal Struggles and Triumphs

Chapter 6
  Political Views
Chapter 7
  Acting and TV Roles
Chapter 8
  Awards and Achievements
Chapter 9
  Health Struggles & Death
  - Diagnosis and Treatment
  - Facing the Brain Tumor
Chapter 10
  Legacy
  - Impact on Literature and Activism
  - Continued Influence

Introduction

In the rhythmic echoes of reggae beats and the profound verses of dub poetry, one name reverberates through the corridors of literary brilliance and social activism—**Benjamin Zephaniah**. As we embark on this literary journey, we are drawn into the vibrant tapestry of a life that transcended words on paper, crafting a legacy that resonates with passion, purpose, and the pursuit of justice.

Benjamin Zephaniah, a name etched in the annals of British literature, stands as a testament to the transformative power of words. In this biography, we unravel the layers of a man who dared to blend poetry with politics, melody with meaning, and who carved a niche for himself in the tapestry of literary history.

Our exploration goes beyond the lines of verse, delving into the roots of Zephaniah's early life, the profound influences that shaped his worldview, and the magnetic pull of poetry that beckoned him into the limelight.

Yet, this biography is more than a chronological account—it is a celebration of a life well-lived. Through personal anecdotes, reflections, and the pulsating rhythm of Zephaniah's own voice, we invite you to witness the man behind the verses, the activist who stood at the intersection of literature and societal change.

As we journey through the pages of Benjamin Zephaniah's life, we uncover not just a literary luminary but a force that stirred the collective conscience, challenging us to rethink, rebel, and reimagine a world where words possess the power to shape destinies.

Join us in this exploration of a life that defied convention, a voice that echoed through the corridors of change, and a legacy that continues to inspire. This is the story of Benjamin Zephaniah—a symphony of words, a melody of activism, and an enduring beacon in the realm of literature.

Chapter 1

Early Life and Background

Childhood and Family

Benjamin Obadiah Iqbal Zephaniah entered the world on April 15, 1958, in Handsworth, Birmingham, United Kingdom. Born into a world of post-colonial transitions, his early years were marked by the echoes of the Windrush generation, a time when the Caribbean diaspora significantly impacted the cultural landscape of Britain.

In the heart of Birmingham, young Benjamin navigated the tapestry of his multicultural neighborhood. His parents, a nurse mother and a postal worker father, provided a foundation steeped in hard work and resilience. It was within the walls of his family home that the seeds of creativity were sown. His mother, in particular, nurtured an environment where curiosity and expression were encouraged, laying the groundwork for the poet-to-be.

Growing up in the midst of societal shifts and cultural diversity, Zephaniah found inspiration in the everyday stories of resilience, community, and the struggles of those around him. The dynamics of his family, woven into the fabric of a rapidly changing Britain, played a crucial role in shaping his understanding of identity, justice, and the power of individual narratives.

Influences and Inspirations

As young Benjamin delved into the literary world, his early influences became guiding stars in his creative journey. The poetic verses of Langston Hughes, the reggae rhythms of Bob Marley, and the revolutionary spirit of the Black Arts Movement in the United States fueled his imagination. These influences, disparate yet interconnected, stirred a passion for poetry and activism within him.

The streets of Handsworth, with its fusion of cultures and languages, became a rich source of inspiration. Zephaniah found poetry in the pulsating rhythms of daily life, the vibrant marketplaces, and the conversations that echoed the struggles and triumphs of his community. This immersion in the tapestry of urban life laid the foundation for his unique voice—a voice that would later redefine the landscape of British literature.

In the crucible of adolescence, Zephaniah's worldview expanded through encounters with the burgeoning punk rock movement. The raw, unfiltered rebellion of punk resonated with his own desire to challenge societal norms and paved the way for the fusion of his poetic expression with unconventional sounds.

The intertwining threads of his cultural heritage, familial roots, and diverse artistic influences wove the intricate fabric of Benjamin Zephaniah's early years. It was a tapestry marked by resilience, creativity, and a profound sense of social responsibility—a tapestry that would lay the groundwork for his emergence as a literary force and a voice for change. As we delve into the depths of his formative years, we witness the genesis of a poet who would go on to challenge conventions, break boundaries, and redefine the very essence of poetry in the context of societal evolution.

Chapter 2

Journey into Poetry

Discovery of Poetry

Benjamin Zephaniah's journey into poetry was not a carefully laid path but a series of serendipitous encounters and personal revelations that unfolded against the backdrop of a changing cultural landscape. Poetry, in its various forms, had been a part of Zephaniah's early life, but it was during his teenage years that he discovered its transformative power.

In the rebellious corridors of adolescence, Zephaniah found solace and expression in the written word. The rhythmic cadence of his verses became a means of navigating the complexities of identity, race, and societal expectations. His early poems, infused with the raw energy of punk and the soulful resonance of reggae, were not merely words on paper; they were a manifestation of a burgeoning voice that sought to challenge and redefine.

The vibrant streets of Handsworth provided a canvas for Zephaniah's poetic exploration. His observations of the urban landscape, the struggles of his community, and the nuances of everyday life became the ink with which he painted his poetic tapestry. It was here that he discovered the power of poetry to serve as a mirror reflecting the realities of the world around him.

As he delved into the works of poets who came before him, Zephaniah's appreciation for the diversity of poetic expression expanded. The lyrical elegance of Langston Hughes, the socio-political commentary of Amiri Baraka, and the poignant simplicity of William Blake each left an indelible mark on his evolving style. These influences, combined with his own lived experiences, fueled the fire of creativity within him.

Development of Dub Poetry

The fusion of reggae beats and spoken word poetry marked a pivotal moment in Zephaniah's artistic evolution, giving birth to what would later be coined as "*dub poetry*." This innovative form of expression emerged organically, a response to the pulsating rhythms of reggae music that echoed the heartbeat of his Caribbean roots.

Zephaniah's encounters with the reggae scene, particularly the dub music subgenre, became a catalyst for experimentation. The marriage of his rhythmic verses with the bass-heavy, dub-infused melodies created a dynamic synergy that transcended traditional boundaries of poetry. Dub poetry became not only a mode of artistic expression but a cultural phenomenon that resonated with audiences far beyond the realms of literature.

The performances of Zephaniah, often accompanied by reggae musicians, transformed poetry from a solitary pursuit into a communal experience. The spoken word, amplified by the beats of reggae, took on a new life—pulsating with the heartbeat of rebellion and social consciousness. It was a marriage of two worlds, an alchemical fusion that breathed life into his words and amplified their impact.

Through the development of dub poetry, Zephaniah pioneered a genre that became a vehicle for social commentary. His verses, now intertwined with the infectious rhythms of reggae, became a powerful medium to address issues of racism, inequality, and societal injustice. The dub poetry movement, with Zephaniah at its forefront, challenged conventions and created a space for marginalized voices to be heard.

In the crucible of discovery and development, Benjamin Zephaniah not only found his poetic voice but also pioneered a genre that would leave an indelible mark on the landscape of literature and music. The journey into poetry was not just a personal exploration; it was a transformative odyssey that reshaped the very contours of artistic expression.

Chapter 3

Literary Contributions

Notable Works:

Benjamin Zephaniah's literary contributions are a vibrant tapestry of words that traverse the realms of poetry, prose, and performance. Each piece is a brushstroke on the canvas of societal consciousness, leaving an indelible mark on the landscape of British literature.

The Dread Affair: Collected Poems (1985):

This anthology stands as a testament to Zephaniah's early poetic prowess. It encapsulates the raw energy of his formative years, exploring themes of identity, love, and the socio-political landscape.

Talking Turkeys and Other Poems (1994):

A collection that combines wit, humor, and poignant social commentary. In this work, Zephaniah employs his distinctive style to address issues such as animal rights, racism, and inequality, using language as a powerful tool for advocacy.

Propa Propaganda (1996):

This collection delves deeper into Zephaniah's exploration of dub poetry, fusing rhythm and verse to amplify his social and political messages. It showcases his ability to seamlessly merge the oral traditions of reggae with the written word.

Refugee Boy (2001):

Venturing into the realm of fiction, Zephaniah's novel tells the story of Alem, a young Ethiopian refugee navigating the complexities of identity and displacement. The novel explores themes of immigration, cultural assimilation, and the human cost of conflict.

<u>Windrush: Songs in a Strange Land (2007)</u>:

A poetic exploration of the Windrush generation, delving into the experiences of Caribbean migrants who arrived in the United Kingdom between 1948 and 1971. Zephaniah's verses pay homage to the resilience and cultural contributions of this generation.

Style and Themes:

Zephaniah's literary style is a dynamic fusion of influences, a harmonious blend of the rhythmic beats of reggae, the raw energy of punk, and the lyrical elegance of traditional poetry. His words are a rhythmic dance on the page, each line pulsating with the heartbeat of social consciousness.

The themes woven into Zephaniah's work reflect the tapestry of his own experiences and the societal landscape he inhabits:

Identity and Cultural Roots:
Zephaniah's explorati on of identity, particularly in the context of his Afro-Caribbean heritage, is a recurring theme. His verses delve into the complexities of belonging, cultural pride, and the intersectionality of identity markers.

Love and Relationships:
Amidst the socio-political commentary, Zephaniah weaves verses that explore the nuances of love and human connections. His poetry is not only a tool for critique but also a medium for celebrating the beauty of human relationships.

Nature and Environment:
Zephaniah's environmental activism finds expression in his works that highlight the interconnectedness of humanity and nature. He

addresses ecological concerns, animal rights, and the impact of human actions on the planet.

In his literary contributions, Benjamin Zephaniah emerges not just as a poet but as a cultural architect, shaping narratives that challenge, inspire, and resonate with the pulse of societal evolution. His unique blend of style and themes continues to leave an enduring imprint on the literary landscape, inviting readers to engage with the world through the lens of poetic expression.

Chapter 4

Musical Pursuits

Integration of Poetry with Reggae

Benjamin Zephaniah's foray into the musical realm was not merely an artistic experiment; it was a revolutionary convergence of poetry and reggae that would redefine the boundaries of both genres. The roots of this integration trace back to Zephaniah's early experiences with the reggae scene, where the rhythmic beats and socially conscious lyrics resonated deeply with his own poetic sensibilities.

In the crucible of Birmingham's diverse music scene, Zephaniah found a natural synergy between the spoken word and the bass-heavy rhythms of reggae. His encounters with reggae artists and musicians became pivotal moments of collaboration and artistic exploration. Inspired by the dub music subgenre, which featured instrumental remixes emphasizing rhythm and bass, Zephaniah saw an opportunity to infuse his poetry with the infectious beats of reggae.

The integration of poetry with reggae was not a mere overlay of words on music but a harmonious fusion where each element enhanced the other. Zephaniah's distinctive vocal delivery, with its rhythmic cadence and melodic intonations, found a seamless partnership with reggae's pulsating heartbeat. The result was a new form of expression—dub poetry—where the power of spoken word merged with the soul-stirring sounds of reggae.

Zephaniah's performances, often accompanied by reggae musicians, created an immersive experience for audiences. The spoken word, elevated by the musical backdrop, transcended traditional boundaries, becoming a communal celebration of both language and rhythm. This integration was not confined to the stage; it permeated recordings, turning albums into sonic landscapes where poetry and reggae coexisted in dynamic harmony.

Impact on the Music Scene

Zephaniah's venture into dub poetry had a profound impact on the music scene, contributing to a paradigm shift in how poetry and activism could intersect with popular music. His collaborations with reggae musicians brought a socio-political dimension to the genre, expanding its scope beyond entertainment to become a medium for social commentary and protest.

The impact of Zephaniah's integration of poetry with reggae resonated not only in the UK but reached global proportions. His work became emblematic of a movement that used music as a tool for activism and consciousness-raising. The fusion of reggae and dub poetry opened avenues for other artists to explore the marriage of spoken word with various musical genres, fostering a new wave of experimentation in the music industry.

Beyond the immediate music scene, Zephaniah's influence extended to a broader cultural context. Dub poetry became a conduit for marginalized voices, a vehicle for expressing the struggles of communities facing social injustice. By blending the rhythm of reggae with the narratives of activism, Zephaniah contributed to a musical landscape that was not only about entertainment but also about social change.

The impact on the music scene was not solely confined to the 1980s and 1990s when Zephaniah emerged as a prominent figure in the dub poetry movement. His legacy continues to inspire contemporary artists who explore the dynamic intersection of spoken word, poetry, and various musical genres. The integration of poetry with reggae, pioneered by Zephaniah, remains a testament to the enduring power of artistic fusion and the ability of music to transcend boundaries, ignite social consciousness, and shape cultural narratives.

Chapter 5

Personal Life

Relationships and Family

Benjamin Zephaniah's personal life is a tapestry woven with threads of diverse experiences, from the dynamics of relationships to the embrace of cultural and spiritual shifts. For twelve years, he shared his journey with Amina, a theatre administrator, marking a chapter of companionship and collaboration. Their partnership, however, faced the crossroads of change, leading to a divorce in 2001. The ebb and flow of relationships became a facet of Zephaniah's personal narrative, shaping the contours of his emotional landscape.

Beyond the complexities of romantic entanglements, Zephaniah's family roots delve into the realm of Christianity. Raised within a

Christian household, the contours of faith and familial bonds left an indelible imprint on his early years. Yet, as with many aspects of his life, Zephaniah's journey took a unique turn, leading him to embrace Rastafari at a young age. This spiritual transition reflected not only a shift in religious identity but also marked a deeper connection with the cultural roots embedded in the reggae rhythms that would later become integral to his artistic expression.

Personal Struggles and Triumphs

Zephaniah's life journey is one marked by both personal struggles and triumphant moments, a testament to the resilience that often accompanies artistic brilliance. His choice to adopt Rastafari came with its own set of challenges and rewards. The spiritual path he embraced offered a framework for cultural exploration and a means of connecting with his Afro-Caribbean heritage.

In the realm of personal challenges, Zephaniah confronted and overcame the grip of cannabis in his thirties. The decision to relinquish this aspect of his life reflected a commitment to personal well-being and a redirection of focus toward clarity and sobriety. It stands as a testament to his ability to navigate personal challenges and make choices aligned with his evolving principles.

The geographical landscape of Zephaniah's life also underwent a transformation. After many years in East London, he embarked on a lifestyle that saw him dividing his time between a village near Spalding, Lincolnshire, and the vibrant metropolis of Beijing, China. This juxtaposition reflects not only a physical shift but also a testament to his curiosity and openness to diverse cultures. Zephaniah, a keen language learner, immersed himself in the study of Mandarin Chinese for over a decade—a pursuit that reflects his insatiable appetite for intellectual exploration.

Triumphs in Zephaniah's personal life extend beyond the confines of relationships and geographical relocations. As a passionate supporter of Aston Villa F.C., he assumed the role of patron for an Aston Villa supporters' website, intertwining his personal interests with a sense of community and shared enthusiasm.

In examining the tapestry of Benjamin Zephaniah's personal life, we encounter a multifaceted individual whose journey is marked by the complexities of relationships, the resilience to overcome personal challenges, and an unwavering commitment to cultural exploration. His life story becomes not only a canvas of artistic brilliance but also a reflection of the myriad experiences that shape a person's identity and contribute to the rich mosaic of human existence.

Chapter 6

Political Views

Zephaniah identifies as an anarchist and actively supported the shift from the first-past-the-post electoral system to the alternative vote during the 2011 referendum. In a 2017 interview, he expressed his perspective on Brexit, emphasizing that although he believes in left-wing reasons for leaving the EU, the manner of departure was flawed.

In December 2019, Zephaniah, alongside 42 other prominent cultural figures, endorsed the Labour Party led by Jeremy Corbyn in the general election. The joint statement highlighted that Corbyn's leadership and the party's manifesto prioritized the well-being of people and the planet over private profit and the interests of a few.

Chapter 7

Acting and TV Roles

Zephaniah had brief roles in various TV programs during the 1980s and 1990s, such as *The Bill* (1994), *The Comic Strip Presents...* (1994), and *Crucial Tales* (1996).

In 1990, he was part of the cast in the film *Farendj*, directed by Sabine Prenczina and featuring Tim Roth.

From 2013 to 2022, Zephaniah portrayed the character of preacher Jeremiah Jesus in the BBC drama *Peaky Blinders*, appearing in 14 episodes spanning across the show's 6 series.

In 2020, he participated as a panelist on the BBC television program *QI*, specifically on the episode centered around the theme of "*Roaming*."

Chapter 8

Awards and Achievements

Zephaniah achieved recognition by winning the *BBC Young Playwright's Award*. Over the years, he has received honorary doctorates from various institutions, including the University of North London (1998), the University of Central England (1999), Staffordshire University (2001), London South Bank University (2003).

On July 17, 2008, the University of Birmingham conferred an honorary doctorate upon Zephaniah. His literary contributions earned him the 48th position in *The Times* list of the 50 greatest postwar writers.

In addition to his accolades in literature, Zephaniah has ventured into the realm of music, releasing several albums featuring original compositions. His musical endeavors were recognized with the *Best Original Song* award at the Hancocks 2008 Talkawhile Awards for Folk Music. This accolade was specifically for his rendition of Tam Lyn Retold, recorded in collaboration with The Imagined Village. Zephaniah, in receiving the award live at *The Cambridge Folk Festival* on August 2, 2008, humorously dubbed himself a "**Rasta Folkie**."

Chapter 9

Health Struggles & Death

Diagnosis and Treatment

In a poignant turn of events, Benjamin Zephaniah faced a formidable health challenge when he received a diagnosis that would significantly alter the course of his life. The revelation of a brain tumor came as a seismic shock, a stark reminder of the fragility of human existence even for someone who had navigated life's complexities with resilience and artistic prowess.

The journey into the realm of medical diagnosis began eight weeks prior to his death. In that span, Zephaniah, who had spent his life crafting verses and challenging societal norms, found himself confronting a foe that transcended the battles fought on the poetic stage. The diagnosis marked a turning point, ushering him into a realm where the language of medicine supplanted the rhythmic cadence of his spoken word.

The treatment journey was not just a physical ordeal but an emotional and spiritual odyssey. Zephaniah, known for his unwavering stance on social justice, now faced a personal struggle that transcended the boundaries of activism. Medical interventions, consultations with specialists, and the intricate dance with uncertainty became integral components of his daily narrative.

The resilience that defined Zephaniah's artistic and activist endeavors now manifested in a different arena—the resilience to navigate the labyrinthine corridors of hospitals, embrace the uncertainty of treatment outcomes, and find solace in the support of loved ones. The treatment protocol, a blend of medical expertise and Zephaniah's own tenacity, became a battleground where hope and healing engaged in a delicate dance.

Facing the Brain Tumor

To face a brain tumor is to confront the fragility of cognition, the epicenter of thought and creativity. For someone whose life had been a celebration of words, ideas, and the power of expression, the prospect of a brain tumor presented a unique challenge—one that extended beyond the physical realm into the very essence of identity and consciousness.

The confrontation with a brain tumor was not merely a medical episode; it was an existential reckoning. Zephaniah, who had harnessed the potency of language to critique, inspire, and shape societal narratives, now grappled with the vulnerability of his own cognitive sanctuary. The poet, the activist, the cultural architect—all facets of his identity were cast under the shadow of this formidable adversary.

As he faced the uncertainty that accompanied each medical update, Zephaniah exhibited a courage that mirrored the tenacity found in his verses. The metaphorical ink that once flowed freely on the pages of his creativity was now transmuted into the medical charts that tracked his journey through the landscapes of diagnosis and treatment.

Facing a brain tumor demanded not only medical resilience but also emotional fortitude. Zephaniah's openness about his health struggles invited not just sympathy but also a collective acknowledgment of the human experience. The poet who had given voice to societal grievances now found his own voice resonating in the broader conversation about health, mortality, and the shared vulnerability of the human condition.

In facing the formidable presence of a brain tumor, Benjamin Zephaniah exemplified a profound unity—the convergence of his public persona with the private battles that defined his health journey. The poetic narrative, now etched with the indelible ink of medical challenges, became a testament to the interplay of fragility and strength, vulnerability and resilience. As he confronted the shadow of the tumor, Zephaniah's journey became a nuanced exploration of identity, mortality, and the enduring spirit that weaves through the tapestry of the human experience.

Benjamin Zephaniah passed away on December 7, 2023, at the age of 65.

Chapter 10

Legacy

Impact on Literature and Activism

The legacy of Benjamin Zephaniah extends far beyond the confines of his mortal years, resonating in the realms of literature and activism where his imprint remains indelible. Zephaniah's contributions to literature are a symphony of words that transcend the traditional boundaries of verse, echoing themes of identity, social justice, and cultural exploration. His impact on literature is not confined to the eloquence of his poetry but is embodied in the very essence of his message—a call for societal introspection, transformation, and empathy.

Zephaniah's literary works, spanning poetry, prose, and even fiction, have left an enduring mark on the landscape of British literature.

Through the vibrant tapestry of his words, he invited readers to confront societal inequities, challenge established norms, and celebrate the richness of cultural diversity. The marriage of reggae rhythms with spoken word, exemplified in his creation of "dub poetry," showcased an innovative fusion that expanded the possibilities of literary expression.

The impact on literature and activism intertwines in Zephaniah's ability to bridge the realms of art and advocacy. His works became a rallying point for those who sought a voice for the marginalized, an anthem for those who believed in the transformative power of words. The resonance of his message, delivered with both lyrical elegance and unapologetic directness, reverberates through generations, inviting readers and activists alike to engage with the complexities of the world and strive for positive change.

Continued Influence

Benjamin Zephaniah's influence did not dissipate with the closing of his life's chapter; rather, it continues to reverberate through the corridors of literature, activism, and cultural exploration. His legacy is alive in the echoes of every reader who finds solace, inspiration, or a call to action within the pages of his works.

In literature, Zephaniah's continued influence is evident in the voices of contemporary poets and writers who draw inspiration from his fearless approach to tackling societal issues. The spirit of "dub poetry" lives on as artists experiment with the fusion of spoken word and diverse musical genres, echoing Zephaniah's boundary-breaking approach. His themes of identity, social justice, and cultural pride resonate in the works of those who, like him, seek to use literature as a tool for change.

On the frontlines of activism, Zephaniah's legacy endures as a beacon for those who advocate for a more just and inclusive society. His unyielding commitment to speaking truth to power continues to inspire a new generation of activists who recognize the power of language in dismantling systemic injustices. The baton of advocacy, passed down by Zephaniah, is carried by individuals and movements committed to amplifying marginalized voices and addressing the root causes of societal inequities.

Zephaniah's influence extends beyond the written word into the realms of music, where his pioneering fusion of poetry and reggae set a precedent for artists exploring the intersection of spoken word and diverse musical genres. The ripple effect of his "Rasta Folkie" persona resonates with musicians who continue to experiment with the fusion of cultural traditions in their artistic expressions.

The impact of Zephaniah's legacy is not confined to a singular medium or moment; it is a dynamic force that evolves with each reader, each activist, and each artist who engages with his body of work. His continued influence is not merely a static homage but an ongoing dialogue with the world, inviting future generations to weave their own narratives, challenge the status quo, and contribute to the ever-evolving tapestry of literature, activism, and cultural exploration. As long as voices rise in solidarity against injustice and creativity is wielded as a tool for transformation, the legacy of Benjamin Zephaniah remains vibrantly alive.

Printed in Great Britain
by Amazon